BEAT IT!

Group percussion for beginners

Evelyn Glennie & Paul Cameron

CARIBBEAN STREET MUSIC

PIANO SCORES

FABER *ff* MUSIC

Sing an' jump for joy

Rhumba ♩ = 144

4

Nobody's business

Banyan tree (waltz)

Banyan tree (mento)

Rivers of Babylon

Beat it!

AFRICAN DANCES

Group percussion for beginners

by Evelyn Glennie & Paul Cameron

Beat it! African Dances is a brilliant resource for both general and more specialized music teachers working with beginner percussion groups. Presenting sixteen contrasting workshops based on four African dances, it provides invaluable material for use with students up to the age of fourteen.

African Dances contains everything you need for group work:

♦ CD with full performances of each piece, backings for performance and demonstrations of every music example in the pack.

♦ Printed melody lines for the pieces, including permission to photocopy for overhead projector or group use.

♦ Piano parts with chord symbols for guitar as an alternative to CD backing.

♦ Four workshops with each piece – sixteen overall – developing a wealth of contrasting rhythmic and tuned percussion techniques.

♦ Helpful guidance on how to learn the tunes.

♦ Assessment guidelines.

♦ Illustrations and guidance on how to hold and play percussion instruments correctly.

♦ Background information on African instruments.

ISBN 0-571-51778-1

BEAT IT!

Group percussion for beginners

Evelyn Glennie & Paul Cameron

CARIBBEAN STREET MUSIC

Complete resource pack

for group use including CD

FABER *ff* MUSIC

Contents

Introduction   *page 3*

Learning the tunes   *page 5*

An introduction to steel pans   *page 7*

1 **Sing an' jump for joy** *Rhumba*   *page 10*

Instrument workshop: Claves & Tumbas   *page 15*

2 **Nobody's business** *Calypso*   *page 16*

Instrument workshop: Maracas & Large drums   *page 21*

3 **Banyan tree** *Mento*   *page 23*

Instrument workshop: Drum kit   *page 28*

4 **Rivers of Babylon** *Reggae, Pop & Ska*   *page 30*

Melody lines   *page 34*

National Curriculum guidelines   *page 44*

Complete rhythmic accompaniments   *page 45*

CD contents   *page 47*

Inserts

CD

Piano scores

© 2000 by Faber Music Ltd
First published in 2000 by Faber Music Ltd
3 Queen Square London WC1N 3AU
Illustrations by John Levers
Music processed by Richard Ihnatowicz
Printed in England by Halstan & Co Ltd
All rights reserved

ISBN 0-571-51957-1

To buy Faber Music publications or to find out about the full range of titles available
please contact your local retailer or Faber Music sales enquiries:
Tel: +44 (0)1279 82 89 82   Fax: +44 (0)1279 82 89 83
Email: sales@fabermusic.com   Website: www.fabermusic.com

Introduction

How to use this book

This book and CD present four Caribbean songs which can be used by both classroom teachers and percussion specialists. It is an extremely versatile resource for music making.

Our aim is to give an approach to discovering rhythm and how it can be used to build up performances. We seek to encourage flexible teaching techniques by matching instruments available to individuals and groups at many levels of musical understanding. The following guidelines explain how to use the book and CD.

How to use the Rhythm Accompaniment Workshops

Workshop learning is at the core of *Beat it!*, enabling students to develop a rhythmic foundation and vocabulary. The Rhythm Accompaniment Workshops offer a step-by-step approach to the *use* of rhythm, primarily through listening. Treat them as versatile 'workstations'. For each song, they can be used individually or together to lead a group through the simple skills essential for understanding rhythm and how it can be used in performance. Each song has three such workshops, developing rhythmic accompaniment ideas to add to the instrumental parts and thus build complete performances. Use them to give rhythmic backing to the songs using hand-held percussion, percussion instruments, vocalizing, movement and body percussion. The techniques explored are effective with small groups or a full class. Each workshop creates a complete accompaniment which can be used separately, or along with the others for that song to build and layer rhythmic accompaniments.

Altogether, these twelve workshops cover many musical topics and constitute a substantial contribution to a music curriculum. We recommend working through them in the order given. Use of the ideas and skills presented in this book in other songs, dances, tunes and with other instruments is encouraged and highly recommended.

How to use the Instrument Workshops

These workshops give the technical and practical skills necessary to perform on the instruments referred to in the Rhythm Accompaniment Workshops. It is important that percussion instruments are correctly held and played if rhythms natural to them are to sound and 'feel' good. Tips and techniques are given to enable students to get the best results from the instruments.

Use these sections alongside the Rhythm Accompaniment Workshops to develop particular instrumental skills required by students within the group. Each session should include work on both rhythm and instrumental skills. The Instrument Workshops may also be used as starting points for further projects, encouraging the group to learn other skills.

How to use the music

Each song is an arrangement of traditional Caribbean tunes that can be played on tuned and untuned percussion instruments. Melody instruments, for example recorder, violin, etc., can be included if available. Scores with piano parts and chord symbols are provided as a separate insert, while the melody lines are included within the main book. You may photocopy the parts where permission is specifically given for your own overhead projector or classroom use only. Try the following:

- Perform Part 1 as a solo melody on a xylophone, glockenspiel or other melodic instrument.

- Perform Parts 1 and 2 as a duet (Part 2 is an easier beginner's part). In the case of *Sing an' jump for joy* and *Rivers of Babylon* perform Parts 1, 2 and 3 as a trio (Part 3 is the easier beginner's part).

- Perform solo, duet or trio, with piano accompaniment. This is given in each score with chord symbols so that guitar and bass accompaniment can also be added to form a band.

- Perform any of the above with the rhythm accompaniments developed in the workshops (the complete rhythmic accompaniments can be found on page 45). The rhythm workshops contain several different projects for each song (see *How to use the Rhythm Accompaniment Workshops*).

- Perform as solo, duet, trio or ensemble with the CD backing (see *How to use the CD*).

How to use the CD

The CD can be used in two ways. First, as a backing track when learning or performing the solo and duet parts on tuned percussion instruments. This could be a stand-alone backing or in addition to piano, bass, guitar and the rhythm accompaniments developed in the workshops. Secondly, every example given in the Rhythm Accompaniment Workshops is recorded for demonstration purposes.

When working with the Rhythm Accompaniment Workshops, observe the following procedure to encourage the habit and importance of listening skills:

- Listen to the song several times in its complete version to familiarize the group with the material to be used.

- Use the CD when indicated in the text.

- Listen to an example several times before asking the group to join in with it. They can then copy and learn it independently of the CD.

- Make listening and playing equally important.

- At the end of the session, listen again to the song in its complete version so that the group can hear its work in context.

- Now experiment with different performances using CD backing tracks and live instruments according to the skills and instrument resources available. Encourage the students to record these where possible.

- Complete CD contents are listed on page 47.

Learning the tunes

Playing position

- Ensure that the tuned percussion instrument is the correct height for good playing posture. Playing melodies is easier and learning quicker if the performer is comfortable and relaxed. The forearms and sticks should be roughly parallel to the floor. Only sit on the floor to play tuned percussion if a cushion is available; players should also be encouraged to keep a straight back.

- Look at the full pitch range of the piece, and stand so that the body and playing-position are central to the highest and lowest notes.

- Stand with the feet comfortably apart so that the body can rotate at the waist and the weight of the body can move on to each leg in turn. This should give flexible movement up and down the keyboard across the full pitch range of the piece.

Sticking choices (use of left and right hands)

- Sticking choices are often overlooked at the early stages when learning melodies. It is important to understand that good sticking choices result in improved pitch-reading accuracy and general melodic fluency. Try to encourage the use of the weaker hand within a coordinated approach to sticking choices.

- In the simplest terms, having played one note with the right hand the next note has the sticking choice of another right hand or a left hand. Obvious, but given that melodies are directional up and down the keyboard, incremental sticking choices through the melody become fundamental to successful reading.

- Thus, playing melodies well on a tuned percussion instrument relies as much on sticking choices as a melody on a recorder, for example, does on fingering patterns.

Getting started

Snare drum pupils graduating to tuned percussion are often brought up with the rule of 'hand-to-hand' sticking (alternating left hand then right hand in strict succession). This is good for developing equal dexterity in each hand but not particularly relevant to the sticking choices required when learning melodies. As an introduction to tuned percussion, first try playing a 'melody' on a drum, as follows:

- Listen to the full performance of any one Caribbean song on the CD a number of times to hear and understand the shape of the melody. Hear also how the melody fits with the accompaniment. Describe and discuss.

- Counting aloud, listen to the CD backing and clap the rhythm of the melody to understand how counting and rhythm fit together.

- When comfortable and relaxed start to play the rhythm of the melody on a drum. First use whatever sticking seems natural. Play a number of times to become relaxed with playing the rhythm. Try using this as a warm-up exercise or as a means of encouraging the weaker hand.

- At the drum try to think through which sticking would work with the melody. Remember that there is a free choice of sticking at a drum but at a tuned percussion instrument there is the consideration of melodic direction, shape and fluency.

- In the same way that we do not cross hands at the drum, try to avoid this possibility when working out sticking for a melody. Two consecutive right or left hands is acceptable.

- Develop the idea of sticking patterns that fit melodic patterns.

- Finally, take these sticking patterns to the tuned percussion instrument and work them into the melodic patterns, slowly, one pattern at a time.

- Build up the melody in stages but don't always start at the beginning. With *Sing an' jump for joy*, for example, it is fun to change the order of the short 'riffs'.

- When all parts of the melody are comfortable at the same tempo then practise playing the whole melody with CD backing.

- Work at playing the piece without stopping as a *skill* in itself.

There's more to learning melodies than correct notes

- This is where learning to *perform* starts.

- The written page is a set of instructions to be interpreted by a performer and communicated to an audience.

- Interpretation is individual reading, but communication is a group activity. At all levels and standards try to encourage *performance* so that this becomes a natural part of music making.

- Make regular use of performance as a feature of all your music-making sessions so that the habit of communication is encouraged. Do not wait until the end of term or a special occasion to perform but include it as part of each lesson or practise session, even if it is just two bars of music. Always imagine an audience in the room.

- Dynamics are an essential part of performance. In *Beat it!*, we have decided not to be prescriptive about the use of dynamics, but to invite creativity within the group. Pupils should be encouraged to discuss the use of dynamics and experiment with a range of performance outcomes.

An introduction to steel pans

The exciting sound of steel pans played in a steel band typifies Caribbean music[†].

The steel band originates from Trinidad, where large oil drums became a substitute for the *tamboo-bamboo* drum and the *bottle and spoon*, instruments used to accompany Carnival.

These days most instruments are not traditional oil drums but carefully engineered musical instruments with 'skirts' to help the sound resonate. They are played with soft sticks made of dowel wood covered in rubber bands, rubber or foam.

Five pitch ranges, or groups, of steel pans have developed:

1 **Soprano**, **Tenor**, **Ping-Pong** or **lead pans** are the soprano voice.
Although in Trinidad they are called 'tenor pans', you could be excused for calling them 'soprano pans' because of their high range.

2 **Double seconds** (a pair of pans) are the alto voice.

3 **Guitar pans** are a tenor voice.

4 **Cello pans** (pronounced 'chello' pans), arranged as three pans, are another tenor voice.

5 **Bass pans**, sometimes called 'boom pans', are arranged as five pans with four notes on each pan. They produce a deep bass voice.

[†] The other traditional Caribbean instruments mentioned in this book are so characteristically associated with certain rhythmic accompaniments that we introduce them at the first appearance of each rhythm.

Playing steel pans

Let's look at how to play the instrument:

- There are two types of strokes possible.

- Both can be used to create a musical line on the pans.

- Avoid striking the rim or the grooving separating the notes as this will deaden the harmonics and resonance; instead aim for the centre of the notes.

1 The **Drop stroke** – a technique for playing a single note.

- Hold a soft pan stick in each hand.

- Slowly and very gently 'drop' the playing end onto a note, using a gentle flick of the wrist. Alternate the hands when you do this.

- Learn to bounce, rather than bash, the stick. The stick must bounce off the instrument to allow it to speak.

2 **Rolling** – a technique for playing sustained notes.

- Keep the wrists together.

- Play one hand after the other in even succession.

- Listen to the sound and only play as fast as is necessary to sustain the pitch.

- Try and achieve even and consistent rhythm and dynamics.

Learning the tunes

A 'rote' aural teaching method is found all over the world in musical traditions from Irish bodhrán to Indian tabla and African drumming. It works well when learning Caribbean music:

- Play a short phrase on the pan.

- Ask your pupil to copy what you have just played until it is properly memorized.

- The 'rote' method will ensure your pupils really absorb their part and, in the long term, it will benefit their playing in a group context.

In Trinidad the pans are also taught in an 'action' method: sheet music is not used and the note names are not embossed on the pans. Players must, therefore, use aural skills to work out a tune.

It may be possible to mix 'rote' and 'action' learning, but whatever you do, always ensure that players in the steel band absorb the melody of the tune, or even better, all the parts that make up the arrangement, into their bloodstream.

Arranging for steel band

All the songs in this book work perfectly well without steel pans. If you are fortunate enough to have access to a few here are some suggestions.

1 The songs can be arranged for a scaled-down ensemble such as a four-piece steel band rather than the more typical ten-piece band. A possible instrumentation could be a lead pan, double second pan and triple guitar pan (three pans, one player), with electric bass and drum-kit.

2 A lead pan alone, playing the melody, even in the presence of only two other pans, can sound weak in certain musical passages. This explains why the large bands of Trinidad and Tobago have such a high lead-pan-to-band ratio. In the songs in this book it may be possible to double the lead pans with another melody instrument, such as a saxophone or flute, and sometimes a double tenor pan (two pans, one player). The timbre of these instruments mixes well with the steel pan and will not only strengthen the melody but also add brilliant colour.

3 Another effective way of strengthening the melody is to use double second pans, normally used to accompany parts in arrangements, as a second melody voice. The double second pan player can double the melody in unison or an octave below the lead pan and then between melody passages, can resort back to the role of accompanist. Traditionally, these accompanying passages are known as 'strumming'. Take care to balance the playing volume, making sure the melody is clearly audible, and back off the 'strumming' where necessary.

4 If you want more emphasis on a relatively short passage, try doubling the melody over a three-octave range. For a more subtle emphasis play the melody at the distance of two octaves using the lead and cello pans.

Sing an' jump for joy

Rhumba

Sing an' jump for joy is an arrangement of a duet in **rhumba** style. There are three short 'riffs' (musical and rhythmical patterns) that can be repeated to create a 'feel' or 'groove', with each identified by the numbers I to III. The piano score of *Sing an' jump for joy* joins all three 'riffs' together into a longer piece. It also includes chord symbols for guitar, etc. For the melody lines see pages 34 to 36.

 ⬚ *Sing an' jump for joy* – the whole piece, full performance.

Using pitch

Parts 1, 2 & 3 are to be played on tuned percussion or melody instruments or can be sung. Parts 1 & 2, the duet parts, follow the same rhythm throughout playing in intervals of a 3rd, a 6th or in unison. Each is to be played on a separate xylophone, or, if performed an octave apart, on the same instrument; two glockenspiels are another alternative. Part 3 is an easier, beginner's part, which functions as a bass line. It can be played lower down on the same instrument or on a second tuned instrument. It may also be transposed to the timpani by a more experienced player, or a bass melody instrument (for example, bass guitar or cello) using the bass clef part on page 36.

Parts 1, 2 & 3 for *Sing an' jump for joy* – see pages 34 to 36.

Learn Parts 1, 2 & 3 with the group. CD tracks ⬚–⬚ will help you do this.

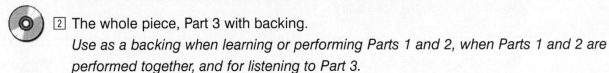

The whole piece, Part 3 with backing.
Use as a backing when learning or performing Parts 1 and 2, when Parts 1 and 2 are performed together, and for listening to Part 3.

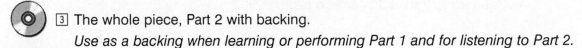

The whole piece, Part 2 with backing.
Use as a backing when learning or performing Part 1 and for listening to Part 2.

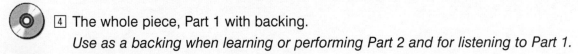

The whole piece, Part 1 with backing.
Use as a backing when learning or performing Part 2 and for listening to Part 1.

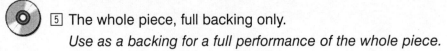

The whole piece, full backing only.
Use as a backing for a full performance of the whole piece.

RHYTHM ACCOMPANIMENT WORKSHOPS

Sing an' jump for joy is a great place to start exploring Caribbean rhythmic accompaniments. First let's address quaver/eighth notes and develop a Caribbean rhythmic foundation ... the **clave** rhythm. ('Eighth notes' are the same as 'quavers'.)

WORKSHOP 1: WORKING WITH QUAVERS/EIGHTH NOTES

Caribbean music offers a wealth of rhythmic accompaniments: **rhumba**, **calypso**, **mento**, **reggae** and **ska** are the most common. Each is different in rhythmic 'feel' but shares a common fundamental 'personality' of quavers/eighth notes. Indigenous rhythmic character and flavour has evolved through the use of different emphases of shape and syncopation to these quaver/eighth note groups.

- First, sit on chairs in a group, possibly in a circle, with both feet comfortably on the floor.

- Someone within the workshop group should now set up a 'pulse', like a clock or a metronome, with their hands 'playing' on to their upper legs. You could use a metronome, although this may not be heard when everyone is working. In any case, it is preferable for the workshop group to 'create' the pulse and therefore feel a responsibility for it.

- Others in the workshop group should now listen carefully to this pulse. When they feel relaxed with its tempo and pace they can join in, placing in rotation their right foot on one pulse and the left foot on the next:

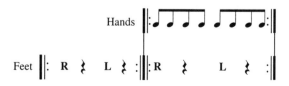

- Use small, relaxed movements for the feet. Keep the heel on the floor and lift the toes; or, keep the front of the foot on the floor and lift the heel.

- Establish a comfortable tempo within the group and ensure the pulse is 'sitting' comfortably.

- When the pulse is comfortable over a considerable number of repetitions, begin to add quavers/eighth notes with your hands 'playing' on to the upper legs:

- Relax the fleshy part of the hands on the upper legs then move the hand up and down from the wrist and play using the fingers. Use small, relaxed hand movements.

- Keep the fingers close to the legs, only lifting them to prepare for the next stroke.

- Use both hands and alternate between them. The quavers/eighth notes should be long and sustained.

- Try to think and 'feel' a continuous sound, and maintain the pattern for a long time to allow this to occur. You should be conscious of eight continuous sounds in repetition and not a rhythm of eight unrelated sounds.

- Whilst playing the quavers/eighth notes and moving the feet, try to allow your thinking and listening to focus on the sound of the whole group and not on your individual playing. Try to 'feel' your body movements as part of an overall 'group sound' and not just of relevance to your own individual notes.

WORKSHOP 2: CLAVE RHYTHM

Continuous groups of quavers/eighth notes are characteristic of Caribbean rhythmic accompaniments. Using various hand patterns and subdivisions it is possible to create a key flavour of Caribbean music-making, the clave rhythm.

- Listen to *Sing an' jump for joy* several times and work out how the quavers/eighth notes in the rhythmic accompaniment are 'grouped' to create a particular rhythmic shape and 'feel'. It is this emphasis on certain quavers/eighth notes within each group that is called a clave rhythm.

- We can create clave rhythm with our hands and feet and establish the rhythmic accompaniment for a rhumba.

- To start, re-establish the hand and feet accompaniment described in Workshop 1. Refer to the second music example on page 11.

 1 Use this rhythmic foundation to accompany *Sing an' jump for joy*. When, after a number of repetitions, you are comfortable and relaxed with the foundation, you could try adding a vocal line on top.

- Rhumba has its roots in Africa; *Sing an' jump for joy* uses a singing style that probably came to the Caribbean from there. A vocalist, called a 'bomma', sings an improvised solo over the rhythms, with the lyrics made up on the spot; these often comment on local incidents and gossip. A vocal chorus sings an answering response. As a further option you could try improvising your own words to the song; make them reflect local issues or classroom stories.

- To copy rhythmic patterns with the voice, use phonetics. These are nonsense words that can recreate the sound of percussion instruments. To begin let's copy a **clave** rhythm. This rhythm is a two-bar shape that 'sits' on top of the hand and feet rhythmic accompaniment. Try saying the following phonetics whilst you play the quaver/eighth notes:

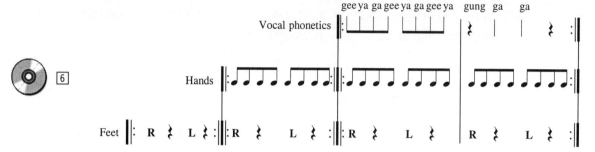

- The phonetics in the first bar copy the rhythm of the quaver/eighth notes. In the second bar they sound longer, as each is sustained through two quavers/eighth notes.

- Emphasize the 'gee' sounds and make the 'gung' sound lower in pitch.

- Make these phonetic sounds long and relaxed and allow them to follow their natural shape and stress; enjoy creating a 'laid-back' and 'under-the-breath' sound.

- When your are comfortable with the combination of feet tapping the pulse, hands playing a quaver/eighth note 'feel', and voice 'saying' a **clave** rhythm, divide the group in half. One group should continue to clap the quaver/eighth note 'feel', while members of the other group, retaining the quaver/eighth note 'feel' in their heads, should clap the **clave** rhythm.

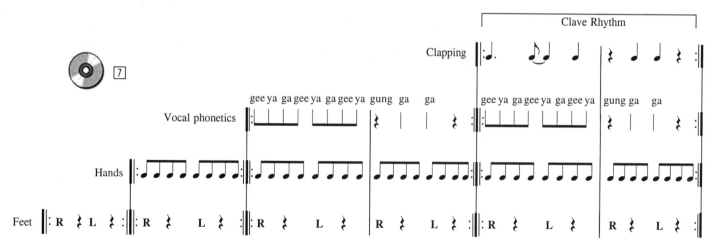

- Listen carefully to your clapping; ensure you produce long, sustained sounds. Keep repeating them until the sound is comfortable and relaxed.

 Finally, stop clapping the **clave** rhythm and instead play it on the claves (refer to the instrument workshop on page 15). Listen carefully and make certain you understand how this rhythm fits with the quaver/eighth notes and the pulse.

WORKSHOP 3: LISTENING TO RHYTHM

Careful, considered listening, particularly to the work of others, should always be stressed to players in a workshop group.

The 'mechanics' of the instruments, their rhythms and the 'orchestration' of sounds all set up a 'feel' and 'groove' – just as the choice, freshness and relative quantities of cooking ingredients can create a fantastic meal!

- Split the workshop group into four 'parts' and build each up in stages:

1 Group 1 play the pulse using their feet.

2 Add group 2 who play quavers/eighth notes with the hands on their upper legs to create a 'feel'.

3 Add group 3, vocalizing the phonetics.

4 Finally, complete the 'groove' with group 4 playing or clapping the clave rhythm.

Refer to the second music example on page 13.

- When the whole group is playing together and relaxed with the sound, ask the different parts in turn to remain silent and 'think' their part rather than actually playing it. The silent group should work through their rhythm in their heads, and understand how it fits the others.

- Encourage the whole group to listen to the range of rhythmic possibilities.

- Play along with track ① on the CD and set up a rhythmic accompaniment to a rhumba. Refer to *How to use the CD* on page 4. Then allow the workshop group to improvise – using the various combinations of feet, and hands clapping the **clave** rhythm – and respond to the changes in 'feel' throughout the song.

- Try working with each 'riff' individually, listening carefully to each group of rhythms. When playing a rhythmic pattern allow your attention to focus on the rhythms happening around you; feel that your rhythm is adding a nuance to the blend of rhythms, not competing with them.

INSTRUMENT WORKSHOP

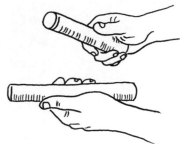

- Claves, two resonant round sticks, make a high-pitched wooden sound when struck together. Each clave is fifteen to twenty centimetres long, two to four centimetres thick, and made from hard wood.

- Place one clave on a cupped hand, along the thumb; use the other fingers to keep the clave safe and steady on the hand. To act as a resonating chamber the hand is cupped.

 8 With the other clave play the rhythm by striking it on the middle of the clave held in the cupped hand. Refer to *How to use the CD* on page 4 and listen to track 8.

- If claves are unavailable, the rhythm can be played on anything made of wood provided it gives a hollow wooden sound – a wood block or temple block is ideal.

- A 'rhumbon' is the name of a gathering where many drums accompany a rhumba. One such drum, the tumba, is a deep-sounding instrument. It provides the foundation of the rhythmic accompaniment group.

- A large box or case is often used to play the 'box rhumba' rhythm. Today there are a range of alternative modern instruments, including some designed for young people to play comfortably.

- Find out from Workshop 4 (on page 16) how to create a basic rhumba rhythmic accompaniment with these instruments.

Nobody's business

Calypso

The **calypso** is a song of scandal and satire, with improvised words. The most popular **calypso** style comes from Trinidad and has the same rhythmical 'style' as the **rhumba**. The **calypso**, however, uses only the first bar of the **clave** rhythm and is therefore a one-bar rhythmic accompaniment. The separate piano score provided also includes chord symbols for guitar, etc. For the melody lines see pages 37 and 38.

 ⑨ *Nobody's business* – the whole piece, full performance.

Using pitch

The two parts are to be played on tuned percussion or melody instruments or can be sung. Part 1 is a melody line, to be played on a xylophone, glockenspiel or other melody instrument. Part 2 is an easier, beginner's part, which functions as a bass line. It can be played lower down on the same instrument or on a second, tuned instrument. It may also be transposed to the timpani by a more experienced player, or a bass melody instrument (for example, bass guitar or cello) using the bass clef part on page 38.

Parts 1 & 2 for *Nobody's business* – see pages 37 and 38.

Learn Parts 1 & 2 with the group. CD tracks ⑩ and ⑪ will help you do this.

 ⑩ The whole piece, Part 2 with backing.
Use as a backing when learning or performing Part 1 and for listening to Part 2.

 ⑪ The whole piece, Part 1 with backing.
Use as a backing when learning or performing Part 2 and for listening to Part 1.

 ⑫ The whole piece, full backing only.
Use for a full performance of the whole piece.

RHYTHMIC ACCOMPANIMENT WORKSHOPS

The calypso uses the 'box rhumba' rhythm introduced on page 18 (here called the **tumbao**) in combination with the **clave** rhythm to build the essential flavours of this song style and one-bar rhythmic accompaniment.

WORKSHOP 4: BASIC TUMBAO RHYTHM (OR BOX RHUMBA)

- The 'box rhumba' rhythm has two distinctive open and closed sounds, made by the hands playing on a box – lots of fun can be had just using a cardboard box!

- Find a good solid box – or if you have a tumba drum play it on that; the 'box **rhumba**' rhythm you then produce will be called a **tumbao** rhythm – and turn it on to its side, or front, to create a playing surface.

First we shall look at the closed stroke.

Hand movement 1: Closed stroke (+)

- For the Closed Stroke the hand should be held slightly cupped with the fingers together and the thumb closed, lying against the side of the hand.
  For a closed stroke the whole hand connects with the drumhead, or box, simultaneously. The wrist is relaxed and the movement of the hand comes from the elbow.

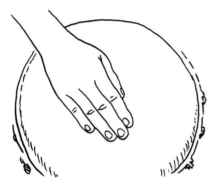 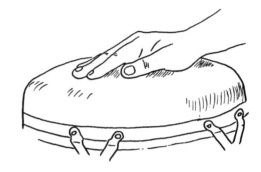

Hand movement 2: Open stroke (0)

- The Open Stroke makes a 'sustained' or hollow sound. The hand is held flat with the fingers together and the thumb out to the side and stretched slightly upwards to prevent it hitting the edge of the drum. The objective is to strike the drum with the fleshy pads at the base of the fingers.

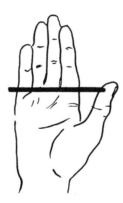

- To ensure a clean open tone, the four fingers should maintain the flat position when they connect with the drum.

- Use the wrist and lift the hand immediately on impact so that the sound is 'sustained'.

- Now, let's set up the tumbao rhythm. In common with the rhythmic accompaniment to the rhumba, the tumbao rhythm fits the foundation of the foot pulse and the quaver/eighth note 'feel' established with the hands:

- One hand plays the closed stroke (indicated in the music by a +); the stronger hand plays the open stroke (indicated in the music by a o). As an alternative, when you are confident and relaxed with the rhythm, swap the roles of the hands around.

rhythm ACCOMPANIMENT WORKSHOP **5**

WORKSHOP 5: LISTENING WITHIN A RHYTHM GROUP

- Split the workshop group between two instruments, one a closed-stroke team, the other an open-stroke team.

- Play the tumbao rhythm and ensure the two teams sound like one player – encourage careful listening and good ensemble skills.

- To help enhance these skills try playing with your eyes shut; the groups will then depend on a secure and confident sense of pulse and 'feel'.

- We can now use the clave rhythm, together with the tumbao rhythm and the hands' quaver/eighth notes, to create a rhumba rhythmic accompaniment for *Sing an' jump for joy*:

- Next apply an almost identical treatment to the calypso song, *Nobody's business*. This time just use the first bar of the clave rhythm, along with the tumbao rhythm and the hands' quavers/eighth notes. Keep repeating them until you create a solid rhythmic accompaniment:

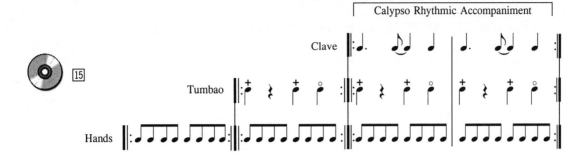

- Listen carefully to the CD and build up the rhythmic accompaniment in stages. Refer to *How to use the CD* on page 4.

WORKSHOP 6: RHYTHMIC 'HARMONIES'

The clave and tumbao rhythms are essential ingredients of rhumba and calypso.

Let's now spice up the sound and play the basic quaver/eighth note 'feel' on hand-held instruments. The quaver/eighth notes function like a harmony, holding a melody (clave rhythm) and bass line (tumbao rhythm) together. Just as songs can often be harmonized a number of ways to create different moods, so too can the clave rhythm be rhythmically 'harmonized' in a range of alternatives to suit the instruments and skills available.

- A popular rhumba and calypso style involves accenting a maraca pattern. Refer to the instrument workshop on page 21. The accents are produced using big forward arm movements synchronized with the 'feel' of the basic rhythmic pattern.

- Improvised hand patterns based on the basic quaver/eighth note 'feel' can be used to vary the rhythmic 'harmonies'. Refer to Workshop 1 on page 11. Let's focus on creating two contrasting sounds when we play the quaver/eighth note hand movements. This time, as an alternative to playing on to the upper legs, play on to your chest.

- Each hand adopts a different movement:

Hand movement 1: Closed stroke (+)

Rest the heel of the hand on the body.

Make a simple, small up-and-down movement from the wrist.

Play on to the chest with the fingers held together.

Hand movement 2: Open stroke (o)

With a flexible wrist, make a substantial hand movement from the wrist and arm.

Play with a cupped hand on to the body.

- Now experiment with the following hand patterns, using one hand for the open sounds and the other for the closed:

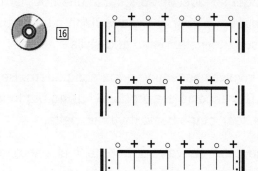

- The open stroke should sound accented and exciting; the closed strokes fill out the remaining quaver/eighth notes.

- Now 'play' the open strokes on any suitable object that comes to hand (a bottle, box or can). Keep the closed strokes confined to the chest.

- Rhythmic 'harmonies' can be improvised on boxes, tins, tabletops and chairs or on your body. Have fun discovering the possibilities!

INSTRUMENT WORKSHOP Maracas & Large drums

Maracas are round or pear-shaped gourds, filled with dried peas or fruit pips. Modern versions exist made of wood, plastic, coconuts or leather. Similar instruments can be made in the classroom by placing dried peas in a hand-held sealed container.

- The basic rhythm for the maracas is the quaver/eighth note 'feel' established in workshop 1. Refer back to this workshop and work at setting up the quaver/eighth note 'feel' on the upper legs. Pay particular attention to your hand movement.

- When playing on the upper legs is relaxed and comfortable, make an identical movement onto a wall facing you.

- Now place a maraca in each hand, holding the instrument upright with your thumbs pointing towards your body.

- Maracas are played with a forward movement away from your body jogging the contents of the maracas sharply against the inside surface of the shell.

- Move each maraca forward one hand at a time.

- The backward movement is relaxed, a preparation for the next forward stroke. The backward movement should as far as possible be silent.

 17 Listen to the sound and the 'feel' of this pattern and aim for a fluent strong sound.

If you do not have a tumba use a large drum in the classroom.

- The large drum can be played with a stick in one hand; the other produces open or closed sounds.

- It is best to use a soft-headed mallet or the blunt end (butt-end) of a drumstick to strike the drumhead.

- The drum can be free-standing, mounted on a stand, or attached by a strap to the performer.

- Make sure you give the drummer plenty of room to move in response to the music.

- There are two different sounds available:

Hand movement 1:   Closed stroke (+)

With one hand placed on the drumhead (the dampening hand) strike the drumhead in the centre with the stick. The dampening hand stays on the drumhead until the next open stroke.

Open stroke (o)

With the dampening hand still on the drum, strike the drumhead in the centre with the stick and then remove it promptly to allow the sound to sustain. Emphasise this stroke within the pattern.

 18 Listen to the tumbao pattern on the large drum. Refer to *How to use the CD* on page 4.

Banyan tree

Mento is a traditional Jamaican song and dance style. It is believed to be a fusion of African rhythm with European melody. In *Banyan tree* a European waltz is given a Caribbean flavour when the rhythm becomes a mento in 4/4 time.

Banyan tree is given here in two arrangements. One is an arrangement in European waltz time, the other a Caribbean arrangement with a mento rhythmic accompaniment. The two arrangements of the same melody can either be worked and performed separately – there are separate workshops to develop the rhythmic accompaniments to each – or, for additional fun, you can experiment with performing them together as a continuous song moving in rotation between the two time signatures. The piano scores include chord symbols for guitar, etc. For the melody lines see pages 39 and 40.

 ⟦19⟧ *Banyan tree* – full performance in 3/4 waltz style.

 ⟦20⟧ *Banyan tree* – full performance in mento style.

Using pitch

The two parts are to be played on tuned percussion or melody instruments or can be sung. Part 1 is a melody line, to be played on a xylophone, glockenspiel or other melody instrument. Part 2 is an easier, beginner's part which functions as a bass line. It can be played lower down on the same instrument or on a second tuned instrument. It may also be transposed to the timpani by a more experienced player, or a bass melody instrument (for example, bass guitar or cello) using the bass clef part on page 40.

Parts 1 and 2, in each version for *Banyan tree* – see pages 39 and 40.

Learn Parts 1 and 2 with the group. CD tracks ⟦21⟧–⟦26⟧ will help you do this.

 ⟦21⟧ The whole piece in 3/4, Part 2 with backing.
Use as a backing when learning or performing Part 1 and for listening to Part 2.

 ⟦22⟧ The whole piece in 3/4, Part 1 with backing.
Use as a backing when learning or performing Part 2 and for listening to Part 1.

 ⟦23⟧ The whole piece in 3/4, full backing only.
Use as a backing when learning Parts 1 and 2 or for a full performance of the whole piece.

 ⟦24⟧ The whole piece in mento style, Part 2 with backing.
Use as a backing when learning or performing Part 1 and for listening to Part 2.

 ⟦25⟧ The whole piece in mento style, Part 1 with backing.
Use as a backing when learning or performing Part 2 and for listening to Part 1.

 ⟦26⟧ The whole piece in mento style, full backing only.
Use as a backing when learning Parts 1 and 2 or for a full performance of the whole piece.

RHYTHM ACCOMPANIMENT WORKSHOPS

The rhythmic accompaniments to Caribbean music are played by a special accompanying group equipped with a fascinating collection of instruments. These rhythmic instruments have a range of characteristics and sounds. Some play the 'bass line', others follow the line and 'personality' of a 'melody', while a third group provides rhythmic 'harmony' sounds.

rhythm **7**
ACCOMPANIMENT
WORKSHOP

WORKSHOP 7: CREATING A 'MUSICAL SCORE' WITH RHYTHMS

The rhythmic accompaniment to *Banyan tree* in 3/4 is an example of an entirely rhythmic 'musical score'. During this workshop we will think about the rhythmic 'functions' of bass, melody and harmony within a musical score and set up and play a group of instruments called a 'drum kit'.

The basic drum kit comprises three instruments: cymbal, snare drum and bass drum. It may be possible to find alternative instruments within the classroom (refer to the instrument workshop on page 28).

In the classroom three players, or groups of players, could take an instrument each and combine them to make a rhythmical 'musical score'. To begin, we shall build a rhythmic accompaniment for *Banyan tree*.

- Listen to *Banyan tree* a number of times. Refer to *How to use the CD* on page 4.

 19 *Banyan tree* – full performance.

 23 *Banyan tree* – full backing only.

- Focus on the bass line, its rhythm and function within the accompaniment. The bass marks out the start of each bar, keeping the whole accompaniment together. Play the rhythm of this line on a bass drum or floor tom. Try playing along with the CD.

- The snare drum plays the rhythm of the harmony. Listen carefully to the harmony chords playing on the second and third beats of the bar and establish how they fit with the bass-line rhythm. The harmony rhythm marks out the time within the bar, working closely with the bass-line rhythm. Add the snare drum to the bass drum, playing along with the CD.

- Now add the icing on the cake, the open and closed strokes of the cymbal, which follow the rhythm and shape of the melodic line.

- To conclude, combine the three instruments of Workshop 7 and play along with the CD. Experiment with rhythmic 'melodies', 'harmonies' and 'bass lines', applying them to the other songs in this book.

WORKSHOP 8: MAKING ACCENTS

There are many ways of giving shape to melodic and rhythmical musical lines.

We shall now look at accents. These are an emphasis, or a stress, given to particular notes within a rhythmic line. Accents can be written into the score – they are usually shown in the following way:

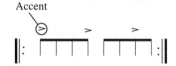

This workshop will focus on developing a 'feel' for their use. The word 'feel' is important here because it suggests an understanding beyond a bland set of instructions on the written page. We shall start with the drum kit rhythmic accompaniment to *Banyan tree* in its 3/4 version set up in Workshop 7.

- In the classroom three players, or groups of players, should take an instrument each and together play the rhythmical 'musical score' described in Workshop 7. This time, play without CD or piano backing. Listen to the sound of the drums and cymbal working together to create a rhythmic line without the support of a melody, harmony or a bass line.

- Although in Workshop 7 we encouraged the drum and cymbal players to follow the rhythm from a musical score, it is also important that they 'feel' and listen carefully to the pitched instruments playing the melody, harmony and bass line.

 19 Listen to *Banyan tree* a number of times.

- Focus on the function and rhythm of the bass line accompaniment. It marks out the start of each bar, keeping the whole accompaniment together.

- Think about the length of each note in the bass line and listen to how it sustains through each bar. Now play the rhythm of the bass line on a bass drum or floor tom, ensuring that each note 'feels' as though it is being sustained through the bar.

- Although the bass drum or floor tom will not 'actually' sustain through the bar, if you apply an accent to the first beat of each bar you will make the listener believe the sustaining is actually happening. Use a bigger stick action to play each note. This will help you get as near as possible to the 'feel' of actually sustaining each note for the length of the bar. Play along with the CD (track 19).

- The cymbal follows the rhythm and shape of the melodic line. Again, try the bigger stick action to achieve a more sustained rhythmic effect. Play along with the CD.

- Apply some of these sustaining ideas to other pieces.

Exaggerated stick movements will benefit a performance, helping you convey a sense (feel) of sustained long notes. Always think about accent, stress and emphasis in terms of 'feel'; such an approach will contribute to a more coherent group performance.

rhythm

9

ACCOMPANIMENT
WORKSHOP

WORKSHOP 9: USING ACCENTS

Caribbean music is a melting pot of rich rhythms. There are many similarities between these rhythms and they represent an interesting feature peculiar to the music of the region. It is, for example, only one accent in *Banyan tree* mento style that differentiates it from its calypso version. It is well worth exploring the subtleties of these distinctive Caribbean song styles. Let's explore some of these rhythmic similarities:

- Popular calypso has the same rhythmical 'style' as the rhumba (refer to *Sing an' jump for joy* on page 10 and the musical example on page 19).

 14 Rhumba rhythmic accompaniment.

 1 *Sing an' jump for joy* – full performance.

- Calypso uses only the first bar of the rhumba clave rhythm and so becomes a one-bar rhythmic accompaniment (refer to *Nobody's business* on page 16 and the musical example on page 19).

 15 Calypso rhythmic accompaniment.

 9 *Nobody's business* – full performance.

- Mento uses all the basic calypso rhythms: quavers/eighth notes combined with the one bar clave and tumbao pattern. Mento style, however, has a strong accent on the last beat of the bar.

Mento Rhythmic Accompaniment

 20 Listen to *Banyan tree* in mento style and establish a tempo and pulse (moving body weight from one leg to the other) in the classroom. Refer to *How to use the CD* on page 4. Move the workshop group into a circle, standing relaxed with feet comfortably apart.

Keep the pulse going and begin a discussion about the rhythmic similarities of the calypso and mento outlined above. Use the same tempo as the CD. Ensure you achieve easy and relaxed movements.

- Keep this movement going for some time and allow the group's concentration to focus on the discussion and not on its body movement.

- Work through in stages building up the basic calypso rhythms with individuals or smaller groups clapping each rhythmic line: quavers/eighth notes first, then the tumbao and, finally, add the one-bar clave rhythm. Refer to the music example on page 19.

- When this is comfortable and relaxed, the group clapping the clave rhythm can add the accent to shift this style into a mento 'feel'. Refer to the music example on page 26.

- Ask the workshop group to repeat this 'feel' many times; then ask it to hum the melody to *Banyan tree* whilst it continues to clap its own rhythm.

- First ask the group to hum each four-bar phrase; make sure everybody is comfortable with each phrase before you move to the next four bars.

- Enjoy the accent and 'feel'. Now work these rhythms through using percussion instruments. Refer to instrument workshops for claves/clave rhythm on page 15, and for maracas (quaver/eighth note rhythm) and large drum (tumbao rhythm) on pages 21 to 22.

Three instruments make up the basic drum kit – cymbal, snare drum and bass drum. Acquaint yourself with the sounds these instruments make and find alternatives in the classroom.

- The **suspended cymbal** can be played with a wooden stick. The stick is held between the thumb and the first joint of the index finger. This finger is bent underneath the beater; the remaining fingers are wrapped loosely around the stick, but do not restrict its movement. Strokes are played using the wrist and the fingers. The left hand controls the use of open and closed strokes. Keep the second finger underneath the cymbal at all times to prevent the cymbal from moving around too much.

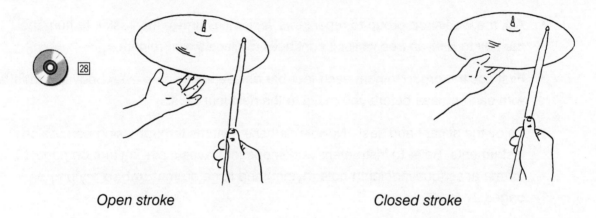

Open stroke   *Closed stroke*

The **triangle**, with its metallic, resonant sounds, is an ideal alternative to the cymbal.

- It is held in the left hand, whilst the right hand holds a metal beater, or vice versa.

- The beater is held between the thumb and the first joint of the index finger, which is bent underneath the beater.

- The strokes are played using the wrist.

- Try some simple rhythmic improvisation using 'open' and 'closed' strokes; these are made using the hand that holds the triangle.

Open stroke

The triangle should hang from the index finger of the left hand or from a small loop of string attached to it and held with the index finger. The fingers are held together and curved at right angles to the hand.

Closed stroke

The fingers and thumb are clenched around the instrument to dampen the sound.

All strokes, whether 'open' or 'closed', are played with the beater. Work out where it should strike the triangle to vary the sound quality. And remember, open strokes will sound louder than closed strokes.

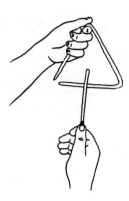

The **snare drum**, played with a wooden stick, is struck on the drumhead. As an alternative, two sticks can be struck together or a whip sound used, created by slapping two strips of wood together.

- The snare drum part could also be played on a **tambourine**. The tambourine is normally held flat with one hand and struck with the palm of the other; although players should be encouraged to experiment with other ways of holding and playing the instrument. Try to discover how many different sounds you can make.

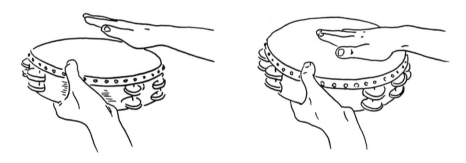

By definition a **bass drum** is a drum pitched lower than the snare drum; it is usually played with a stick. It may also be a hand-held drum played with one stick in the other hand – make this a resonant sound.

- You could play the bass drum part on any large drum. Strike the drum with the fingertips removing them promptly to allow the sound to sustain.

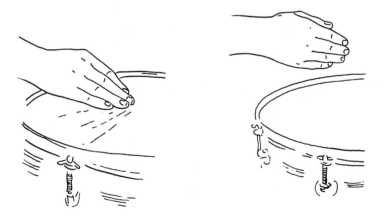

Rivers of Babylon

Reggae and ska are Caribbean styles originating from the rhythm 'n' blues of North America. The main feature of these styles is 'back beat'.

 29 *Rivers of Babylon* – full performance.

Using pitch

Parts 1, 2 & 3 are to be played on tuned percussion or melody instruments or can be sung. Parts 1 & 2, the duet parts, follow the same rhythm throughout. Each is to be played on a separate xylophone, or, if performed an octave apart, on the same instrument; two glockenspiels are another alternative. Part 3 is an easier, beginner's part, which functions as a bass line. It can be played lower down on the same instrument or on a second tuned instrument. It may also be transposed to the timpani by a more experienced player, or a bass melody instrument (for example, bass guitar or cello).

Parts 1, 2 and 3 for *Rivers of Babylon* – see pages 41 to 43.

Learn Parts 1, 2 and 3 with the group. CD tracks 30 – 33 will help you do this.

 30 The whole piece, Part 3 with backing.
Use as a backing when learning or performing Parts 1 and 2, when Parts 1 and 2 are performed together and for listening to Part 3.

 31 The whole piece, Part 2 with backing.
Use as a backing when learning or performing Parts 1 and 3 and for listening to Part 2.

 32 The whole piece, Part 1 with backing.
Use as a backing when learning or performing Parts 2 and 3 and for listening to Part 1.

 33 The whole piece, full backing only.
Use as a backing for a full performance of the whole piece.

RHYTHM ACCOMPANIMENT WORKSHOPS

In rhumba, calypso and mento song styles, 'feel' has been created using the clave and tumbao rhythms and continuous quaver/eighth note patterns with accents. For the indigenous pop music of Jamaica the 'back-beat' is the important flavour.

rhythm **10**
ACCOMPANIMENT
WORKSHOP

WORKSHOP 10: CREATING 'BACK-BEAT'

Back-beat is a very exciting 'feel'. *Rivers of Babylon* gives us an opportunity to experiment and emphasize this 'feel' and create reggae, pop or ska song styles which are usually associated with the drum kit. Refer to the instrument workshop on page 28. Again, quaver/eighth notes feature in all three styles.

- Encourage the workshop group to sit comfortably on chairs with their feet on the floor and legs free to move.

- Set up quavers/eighth notes with the right hand 'playing' on the side of the upper leg. Refer to Workshop 1 on page 11. Keep the wrist and fleshy part of the thumb in constant contact with the leg, lifting just the fingers to 'play' quavers/eighth notes.

- Count aloud four beats in a bar. Keep this vocalization relaxed and under the breath. Make the sounds long and fill each beat with a sustained count.

Keep the base of your hand in contact with your leg. This will ensure confident and secure quavers/eighth notes. It will also mean that the hand can remain relaxed enough to play relaxed-sounding notes. (The right hand is specified here for right-handed players. This, of course, can be changed to the left hand – also, the right foot changed to the left foot if preferred.)

- Now let's add the right foot 'playing' on the first and third beats (the front-beats) of the bar. Keep the toes in constant contact with the floor, lifting only the heel in time to 'play' on the front-beat of the bar.

- The left hand will 'play' the back-beat, beats two and four. Play them with a full arm movement on to the upper leg. Allow the full hand to connect with the leg and play with conviction.

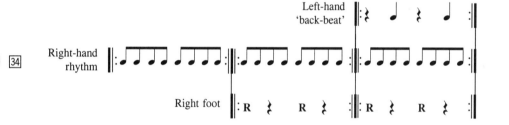

 34

As an alternative try playing the back-beat on a hand drum, or a tambourine placed head-side down on your lap. The left hand should make the same full movement, the full weight of the hand giving a full-bodied sound on the drum head. The drum head is also known as the 'skin'.

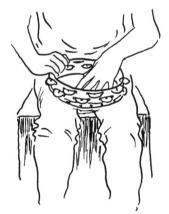

If a drum kit is available in the classroom, place a stick in each hand, between your thumb and first finger, and sit at the drums with your right foot on the bass drum pedal. Establish a pop drums 'feel' and play the right-hand rhythm on a cymbal, and the left-hand 'back-beat' on a snare drum. If a drum kit is not available the hand and feet movements described in the previous workshop will suffice.

29 Listen to *Rivers of Babylon* a number of times and explore the above suggestions with the CD. Refer to *How to use the CD* on page 4.

rhythm

ACCOMPANIMENT
WORKSHOP

WORKSHOP 11: BACK-BEAT POWER

It's now time to explore the 'feel' of the back-beat.

We shall use a similar set of hand and feet movements to those in Workshop 10.

[29] Listen to *Rivers of Babylon* a number of times.

- Playing along to the CD, set up the right-hand quavers/eighth notes and the right foot on beats one and three.

- Keep counting in your head. When relaxed and comfortable try placing the back-beat, with the left hand, on beat three.

- Be aware of how the back-beat on beat three changes the character of the song. This change creates reggae 'feel'. The tempo of the song has not changed, but the emphasis or stress of the back-beat on beat three gives a more laid-back style.

[35]

- Stop, relax and, as an alternative, try placing the back-beat, with the left hand, on to the second quaver/eighth note of each beat. Play along with CD track [36] and listen to how this change in the bar makes a difference to the character of the song. This change sets up a ska 'feel'.

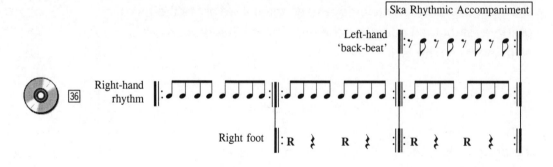

[36]

12

WORKSHOP 12: PUTTING IT ALL TOGETHER!

Tempo, back-beat and 'feel' are all fundamental to the the drummer. The following ideas should help you familiarize yourself with them:

1 Have fun applying the back-beat to other songs.

2 Clap a back-beat to songs on the radio, television or in the pop charts.

3 Sing or hum tunes, 'playing' a back-beat on to your upper legs, or any hand-held percussion instruments.

4 Walk to the tempo of a song (one step to each beat) whilst clapping a back-beat.

5 Beating your hands on your legs, and your feet on the floor, copy various drum rhythms. Have fun making subtle changes to the placing of the back-beat.

Sing an' jump for joy

Part 1

Part 2

Sing an' jump for joy

Rhumba ♩ = 144

Sing an' jump for joy

Rhumba ♩ = 144

Riff I (Bars 1-8)

Riff II (Bars 9-16)

Riff III (Bars 17-24)

Part 1

Nobody's business

Nobody's business

Part 1

Banyan tree (waltz)

Banyan tree (mento)

Banyan tree (waltz)

Banyan tree (mento)

Part 1

Rivers of Babylon

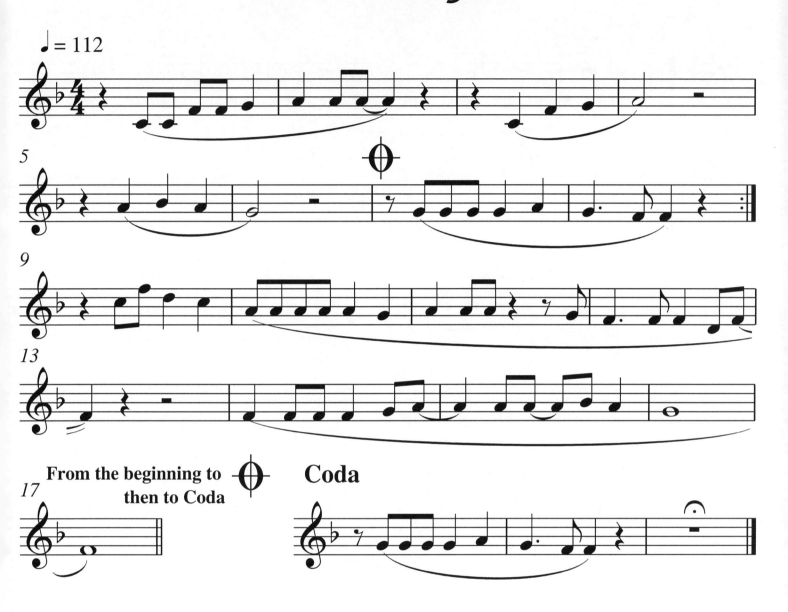

Rivers of Babylon

Part 3

Rivers of Babylon

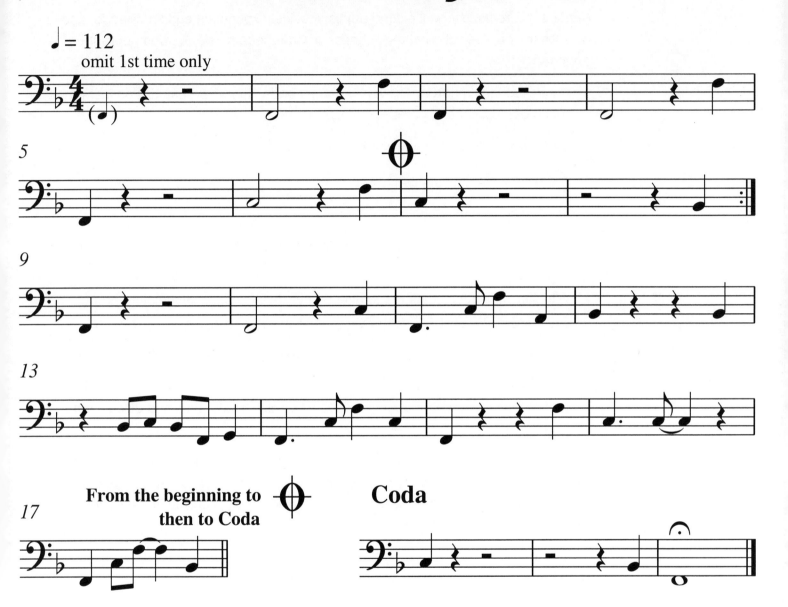

National Curriculum guidelines

Overview

Caribbean Street Music will extend pupils' musical experience and knowledge, and develop their appreciation of the richness of Caribbean music. It gives pupils the opportunity to:

- control sounds made by the voice, hands, body, hand-held percussion instruments, tuned percussion and percussion instruments

- perform and develop an awareness of others

- explore a range of resources

- communicate musical ideas to others

Caribbean Street Music also encourages pupils to use sounds and respond to music through:

- listening with concentration and attention to detail and understanding through exploring, identifying and developing musical ideas

- 'internalizing' rhythmic shapes and percussive sounds in the Rhythm Accompaniment Workshops

- performance which allows the pupils to recognize, distinguish and discriminate between separate musical elements

Caribbean Street Music can develop a pupils' understanding and enjoyment of music. The elements of accompaniment workshop and performance bring together requirements from performing, composing, listening and appraising as specified in the National Curriculum.

Assessment

Satisfactory achievement will have the following qualities:

Key Stage 1
Pupils play pieces and workshop accompaniments with confidence and awareness of pulse. They will explore, select and order sounds. Pupils respond to pieces recognizing repetition and rhythmic shapes.

Key Stage 2
Pupils perform accurately and confidently, making expressive use of rhythmic shape and showing awareness of phrase. They maintain independent rhythmic and instrumental lines with awareness of the other performers in the workshop group. They select and combine appropriate resources, use musical structures and symbols when performing and communicate musical ideas.

Pupils begin to recognize how music is affected by place. They listen with attention to detail and describe and compare music from different traditions, using a musical vocabulary.

Key Stage 3

Pupils perform individual parts with confidence and control, and interpret the mood or feel of the piece. They show awareness of other performers and fit their own part within the whole. They develop musical ideas within structures, using different textures and percussive sounds.

Pupils respond to the pieces, identifying conventions used within different styles and traditions. They use a musical vocabulary appropriately.

Exceptional performance may be identified as:

Pupils who direct others in group performances and/or perform a solo part in a group, demonstrating a sense of ensemble and recognizing when to take the lead and when to support others. They develop musical ideas exploring structures and exploiting a range of resources.

Pupils identify resources used in *Caribbean Street Music*. They identify continuity and change within a range of musical traditions from Caribbean culture, making connections between the music and its cultural context.

Complete rhythmic accompaniments

Clave rhythm (page 13)

Rhumba rhythmic accompaniment (page 18)

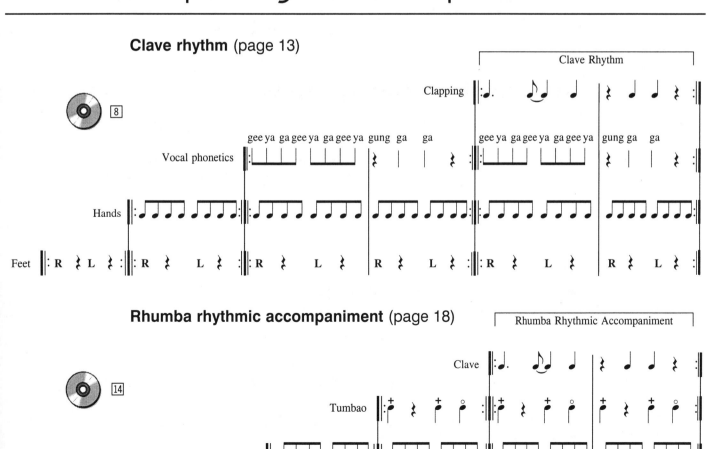

46

Calypso rhythmic accompaniment (page 19)

Mento rhythmic accompaniment (page 26)

Pop rhythmic accompaniment (page 31)

Reggae rhythmic accompaniment (page 32)

Ska rhythmic accompaniment (page 32)

CD CONTENTS

Sing an' jump for joy

1	The whole piece, full performance	1'29
2	The whole piece, Part 3 with backing	1'28
3	The whole piece, Part 2 with backing	1'27
4	The whole piece, Part 1 with backing	1'27
5	The whole piece, full backing only	1'27
6	Adding vocal phonetics	0'23
7	Clapping clave pattern	0'30
8	Clave pattern	0'28

Nobody's business

9	The whole piece, full performance	1'00
10	The whole piece, Part 2 with backing	1'01
11	The whole piece, Part 1 with backing	0'59
12	The whole piece, full backing only	0'59
13	Tumbao pattern	0'22
14	Rhumba rhythmic accompaniment	0'21
15	Calypso rhythmic accompaniment	0'21
16	Open and closed hand-on-body rhythms	0'25
17	Maracas playing quavers/eighth notes	0'19
18	Large drum playing tumbao pattern	0'22

Banyan tree

19	The whole piece, full performance in 3/4 waltz style	0'25
20	The whole piece, full performance in mento style	0'29
21	The whole piece in 3/4, Part 2 with backing	0'24
22	The whole piece in 3/4, Part 1 with backing	0'25
23	The whole piece in 3/4, full backing only	0'24
24	The whole piece in mento style, Part 2 with backing	0'32
25	The whole piece in mento style, Part 1 with backing	0'28
26	The whole piece in mento style, full backing only	0'31
27	Mento rhythmic accompaniment	0'20
28	Open and closed cymbal in 3/4	0'19

Rivers of Babylon

29	Rivers of Babylon, full performance	1'23
30	The whole piece, Part 3 with backing	1'22
31	The whole piece, Part 2 with backing	1'21
32	The whole piece, Part 1 with backing	1'23
33	The whole piece, full backing only	1'19
34	Adding 'pop back-beat'	0'25
35	Adding 'reggae back-beat'	0'25
36	Adding 'ska back-beat'	0'24
	Total timing	33'54

Beat it!
AFRICAN DANCES

Group percussion for beginners

by Evelyn Glennie & Paul Cameron

Beat it! African Dances is a brilliant resource for both general and more specialized music teachers working with beginner percussion groups. Presenting sixteen contrasting workshops based on four African dances, it provides invaluable material for use with students up to the age of fourteen.

African Dances contains everything you need for group work:

- CD with full performances of each piece, backings for performance and demonstrations of every music example in the pack.

- Printed melody lines for the pieces, including permission to photocopy for overhead projector or group use.

- Piano parts with chord symbols for guitar as an alternative to CD backing.

- Four workshops with each piece – sixteen overall – developing a wealth of contrasting rhythmic and tuned percussion techniques.

- Helpful guidance on how to learn the tunes.

- Assessment guidelines.

- Illustrations and guidance on how to hold and play percussion instruments correctly.

- Background information on African instruments.

ISBN 0-571-51778-1

All music written and performed by Paul Cameron.
Piano: Richard Harris
Producer: Kathryn Oswald
Recorded and engineered at Heritage Studio (Engineer: Greg Malcangi)
Ⓟ 2000 by Faber Music Ltd
Ⓒ 2000 by Faber Music Ltd